This Passing Fever

1918 Influenza Poems

Melanie Faith

FUTURECYCLE PRESS
www.futurecycle.org

Library of Congress Control Number: 2017950805

Published by FutureCycle Press
Athens, Georgia, USA

ISBN 978-1-942371-37-3

For my family and my students
who inspire and keep me on this writing path.

Contents

Part One: The First Wave

Part Two: Keep-Away Signs

Part Three: Good Samaritan

Acknowledgments and Historical Notes of Interest

Part One: The First Wave

Rope

"I had a little bird
And its name was Enza.
I opened the window and
In-flew-enza."
—1918 schoolyard rhyme

Plaits slap
a braided smack
against her back
in time to her two
cobbled, lace-up boots
passed down
from her elder sister, Rose.

The rope is a thick twisting,
twined fibers
that make a brush burn
in two pairs of tiny hands
that tick-tock like a clock.
One classmate
at each end, turning, turning.

I had a little bird.
The rhythm
Alma Donovan's heart makes
as classmates call out—
jump in!, jump out!,
jump in!, jump out!—
tiny voices
sing a song of staccato
merriment.

In-flew-enza.
Inside the class:
ten filled inkwells,

ten empty desks,
three students
won't be back
from recess.

Returned

Walter Thornton

His man scent:
tobacco and excitement.

He has been on a big boat
on bigger water.

He has eaten things unpronounceable
and had an aching belly from eating none.

His boots make
exclamation point!, exclamation point!, halt.

It Was There

It was there
when Rose coughed
over her plate
of green beans and ham hock,
with the cadets burning dung
at Camp Funston.

You Are There: March 23, 1918

Camp Funston, Kansas

Picture
the filth
under government-issue boots
after drills in flat fields—
teeth-chattering cold one day,
dust storms the next.

Picture
you'd never had
green bean casserole
that your mother hadn't made.
The fourth son of seven boys
and three girls on a 500-acre homestead,
you'd never seen a skyscraper,
heard French spoken with silent *t*'s,
been off the farm for more than
a night at your cousin's
to bale hay.

Picture
KP duty, march, march, inspection:
pressed slacks, hospital corners,
"yessir, no sir. Louder, cadet!"
Three hots and a cot,
life out of a rucksack, "Taps."
Awaiting a letter from your father,
a package of cookies from
your sweetheart,
Ruby or Helen or Violet.

Walter Thornton

At the table, drop-dough biscuits:
he can eat six at a clip
unlike Walter Junior, James, and Joseph,
his sons in stair steps.
The baby, Thomas, on mother's lap.

Thomas can walk and talk some now
but he is shy with this stranger
who fills the kitchen with voice-noise,
with long, long legs. Thomas does not care
that Walter Junior, James, Joseph, Mommy,
even Lillian ran
to this man's hug.

Mommy does not stop smiling:
Daddy's chair is filled. "At last," she says.
James put Daddy's big woolen war coat
over his head before bed
last night. Draped like a blue ghost,
he bounced from cot to cot
in the big boys' room upstairs

until mother scolded him.
"Quit your foolishness now!"
Lillian, little mother, imitated her
with a finger waggle
at those wild, wily boys.
Dad, behind her,
filling up the doorway,

broad laughing shoulders,
eyes a dove gray.

It Was There When Walter Crossed the Atlantic

in the big boat
and the workers
met the boat at the dock
to take away the already gone.
It followed them to base camp
without taking a step on its own.

Hogs: A You-Are-There Poem, 1904–1918

"It likely started at a pig farm in northern Kansas,
jumping adeptly from hogs to humans as influenza
is known to do." —Kristin A. Watkins, MBA, Holland
Regenerative Medicine Program, University of Nebraska
Medical Center, Omaha, Nebraska

Picture
an earth-tremble of grunts,
assembled willy-nilly, the porcine
shoving snouts out of the way
for the best trough spots,
which are whichever spots you've just
spilled the slop from a dented pail.

From ages 4 to 18
you wake on the bottom bunk,
your brothers elbow and poke you
to pull your boots on in the dark.
You're already in the barn
when the roosters crow from fence-posts;
you've already put in almost two hours
work before your walk to school.

Before breakfast
you stand ankle-deep in the pen
emptying corn mush, pigs jostling into you.
You call: "Step aside now, step aside,"
to which one you cannot say,
as their breath steam-clouds and hangs
in chill morning air. They breathe out
as you breathe in.

The First Wave

1958 Oral History Interview Project,
A Report for Miss Sophokill's Class by Marcus,
Alma Donovan-Smith's Grandson

That first wave
neither of my sisters
came down with it.

But a few boys
and girls in my class did.
Mable Young
put her head down
during Penmanship
and her father had to come for her
that afternoon.

I was seven,
just a couple years younger than you.

Night

Walter thrashes. The bedsheets
tangle at his feet.
He is a cry of throat-
gnashes.

He is back there,
she knows. Across the sea,
in the trenches with rats, mud,
the swamps of green, murky gasses
she read about in newsprint, worried
her knitting needles into heavy socks,
a way to make her fear
he'd come back dead or maimed
into something
sturdy, useful, warm.

Send him home,
home, home safe her every knit one,
purl one. Slipped stitches
she counted back and tore open, trying
not to imagine the corollary:
the body of the Nelson boy in the coffin,
the war medal pinned to his chest.
The hidden gash under the ribs
where the bullet went in,
the Morgan neighbors said.

But Walter's home,
she tries to smile,
her palm itches to touch him,
to mop his brow, to stop him
in the grips.

Nurse Noonan

1933

Leaden with fever,
their eyes—
hazel, grey,
black, blue,
brown, green—
plead
from beds,
from wheelchairs,
from the hospital patio.

No matter that
Roosevelt's on the radio now,
that this patient is her Stella
whose fever will break by morning
in her room with pretty
pink rosebud wallpaper,
the lamp by her bed
left warm and glowing.

In the room:
it's 1918; it's always 1918,
she's failed
to save them.

Quarantine

Hers was the only knock
on many a door.

Minerva took no sign for an answer—
QUARANTINE
INFLUENZA
KEEP OUT OF THIS HOUSE.
She stopped by anyway.

Good Samaritan with chapped cheekbones
and wire-frame glasses, she set to work:
tied an apron
she'd once sewn with her mother.
Life member of the Grant Street Presbyterians,
her wisps of gray hair
the only neighbor's face
they'd seen all week.
More than once,
hers was the last face they'd see.

Bracing wind from her overcoat
floated
atop their beds.

Delusion

Alma

The pearly tooth spikes
     approach first

then panther
claws three inches
long,   long,   long,

     sharp sharp spikes bared.

She bats
the   fur,
the   paws,
the   ears

but the cat springs closer stronger

into her bed
     her red blood
drips

from   clenched jaws

she screams
without   sound,
     with   extreme effort,
she lifts

her arms
her heavy, heavy, heavy arms—

she strikes back.
Once.   Twice.
Again.

The Panther

1958 Oral History Interview Project,
A Report for Miss Sophokill's Class by Marcus,
Alma Donovan-Smith's Grandson

Another time, my mother
brought me a cold compress.
Her raven hair swept up in a comb
became a black panther
with snarling fangs, ready to strike me
in my bed.

I fought her; I'm ashamed of that, but
in the delirium,
I wouldn't let that cat bite into me.
For some reason, my sister Rose
never scared me. Mama had her mind me.

Things got so bad,
even in a town as small town as ours,
there wasn't time for any funerals—
Father Costas at St. Mary's, Pastor Glynn,
Minister Edwards at First Baptist,
they couldn't conduct that many services.

Night, Unending

Walter and Flossie Thornton

He is a mumble of jumbled
orders, an anguished cry.

Tomorrow, he will muck stalls,
pump water from the well,
and she will stand proudly at the window
watching the sinewy ropes, the muscles
of his strong shoulders she fell in love with.
At work, you'd never know he'd been gone.
She will not risk asking him the cost,

what has been lost inside him. In the dark,
his knees jerk, and she turns, counts
his cries, his head thrashing
against the pillowcase
once, thrice, more—she counts
the stars outside the window, their hard cold
spangles cutting into the black—
four, eight, twelve.

His hand flails, a crow,
fingernails
beak-hard against her skin, more mumbles.

She holds back a cough, doesn't know
whether to press closer to his anguish to calm it
or further from the mattress center.

*He is home, home, home
safe,* a litany
with each star.
Thirteen, fifteen, twenty, more.
His torso twists but is not stilled;
she starts over, she starts over.

Calloway's Green Grocery

Tom Heneckle, Commemorative Interview,
The Greenfield Gazette, 1928

Louise and I moved here in '07.
This town's been real good
to me and my family;
even in the hard times, and '18 was
the hardest time the store's seen.

What we missed most
was seeing our neighbors and our friends.
Ask anybody: our soda fountain,
the front porch, the front counter—
we're a meeting place.

Young, old, ditch digger or mill owner—
if you want to bring the kids and wife
to town on a Friday or Saturday,
you'll start at Calloway's,
and we're mighty glad to serve
the community. I tell you, though:
when that influenza swept through,
you couldn't find no community left.

You Are There: April 15, 1918

Camp Funston, Kansas

Picture: thousands
of horses and mules produce
nine tons of manure a month;
you take your turn burning refuse
in a driving wind. Enmeshed in
a putrid yellow haze.
Six weeks ago, you signed up
to fight overseas, now you're burning
smoldering refuse in a pit.

Picture the scent you're missing:
iris, new-sprung daffodils
in the front yard outside the brick
farmhouse where your mother
gathered the seven siblings
together for a parting picture
from an uncle's camera.
A hero's farewell.

The Bells

1958 Oral History Interview Project,
A Report for Miss Sophokill's Class by Marcus,
Alma Donovan-Smith's Grandson

There were bells
in the evening. Pastor Glynn
at the Presbyterian Church on Main
struck one bell
for each report of the stricken.
We lived two blocks away
in a rental house that belonged
to Mama's cousin.

Mama made us
stay quiet when the bells sounded.

We stared down into our plates
of green beans and ham hock.
It was terribly sad. Some poor souls
lost both parents
within days.

It wasn't uncommon for the bells to ring solid
for eight or ten minutes.

It Was There in the Soldiers

who met the French at Brest. There
at the Hindenburg Line,
when they chased the Germans
clutching the sights of hard weapons, aimed
ahead in the murky fortress tunnel.

Part Two: Keep-Away Signs

Enough to Last the Winter

Elmer Canton's wife, Bernice,
the secretary at the primary school,
waved hello to Norman Peters
as she collected mail at the box.
The young man smiled on his porch

when she waved a letter from her sister,
Elsie. "She just canned one hundred more
jars of jam. Enough to last the winter!"
Norman Peters, home from the mill
for the afternoon, called back:
"Delicious. I could surely eat some jam
on homemade bread."

The neighbors parted. *I should take him
some strawberry preserves,* Bernice thought,
then thought no more of it.

Felled

Mrs. Marks said they met
for their usual Tuesday Whist game
while the children were in school.
By Mrs. Thornton's turn, three players
were overtaken.

"We weren't halfway through the round,"
Mrs. Marks shudders,
"when they laid their faces on the tabletop."

Neighbors

Bernice and Elmer Canton

The morning after the jam conversation,
the coroner's wagon parked next door.
She called Elmer to the window.
Who could it be? Norman and his wife
were newlyweds. Norman worked fifty hours
a week. No children yet.

"Must be the grandmother," Elmer said
standing behind Bernice with his hands
on her shoulders. They watched through glass.
They trembled as the stretcher took
Norman Peters out, feet first.

The Comfort of Strawberry Preserves and Toast

Bernice Canton, staring into her supper plate,
while the bells sound

Why didn't I
take preserves to him
last night?

Norman could have enjoyed it.
He could have found
the comfort
of strawberry preserves and toast.
I would never have missed one jar.

Ding—

Now this is just a smear on toast.
now this is just a meaning-to
with no follow-through.

Ding—

Who has an appetite?
He was so young! Too young to go.
Any other time, I would have
taken it over while
soup for Elmer simmered.
Any other time.

Ding—

Just a smear on toast.
So young! Why? He'll never know
the joy of watching his child's first steps,
he'll never hold a grandchild in his arms.
He could have found comfort.
After this, who has an appetite?

Homily

Father Costas

The hand of our Lord works
in mysterious ways.

A barn burns down,
killing the herd
and destroying a year's yield.
But neighbors help rebuild,
bring weeks of meals
until next year's harvest.

A father loses his job
at the foundry, but
he picks up hours
at the mill and maybe
he likes the work better.

A broken engagement
and a parishioner
who cannot imagine how
he'll get out of bed
meets the new schoolteacher
at the ice cream social.

Can we wrap our minds
around not knowing why?
Not on human understanding.
Can we survive in the grips of pain,
thrive in the throes of uncertainty?
With faith. Only with faith.

You Are There: April 20, 1918

Camp Funston, Kansas

Picture 9:00 a.m.:
the kid from Alta Vista
gets the chills,
cannot make his legs walk.

Two hours later:
the guy from Centralia
complains of achy joints, doubles over
in the middle of laps.
He falls, gets punished with detail
he never completes.

You Are There: April 21, 1918

Camp Funston, Kansas

Picture after lights out:
your new best buddy
from Uniontown,
you call him Brush
since he was last in line
at the camp barber,
wakes, afraid
the tent wall is a UFO.

"The aliens are infiltrating!"
he's murmuring.
Your shhhing him, you're shaking—
cold sweat pools in your pits.

He's gone mad.
Your C.O. will hear him,
ship him home, somehow blame you.

"The wallpaper has ears," Brush says.
What wallpaper?
He won't listen. "Their rays
will shoot you dead," Brush warns,
his eyes flaring. What will happen
to your friend? "Stop them,
Stop them!"

Baskets

Tom Heneckle, Commemorative Interview,
The Greenfield Gazette, 1928

Many afternoons
Louise and I were lucky
to see three customers. We spent days
wiping down counters, restocking,
looking for the door to swing open
and a friendly hello. Any hello.

First I shut down
on some weeknights.
Then I stopped ordering
and started delivering perishable
baskets of goods to townsfolk,
friends who could use them.
I tell you, though: people were so scared
wouldn't anybody open their doors. I'd just
leave 'em on the porch and go.

Want Ad*

*My daughter will die
for need of a Nurse.
Won't a Nurse please
come at once: salary
$50.00 per week. 1214
West Lanvale street.*

*Actual want ad from a 1918 newspaper.

Mrs. Myra Marks

I almost went down there
to demand he stop this

ding-ding-ding every evening.
It's downright wrong! It upsets people.

When I'm scouring the supper pots,
and the bells start up, my youngest runs in,

clings to my knees, "Mama. What's that?"
Ding-ding-ding. Minutes on end. Ding-ding-ding.

Who could concentrate with this constant din?
Pastor Glynn and his bells!

Frank stopped me in the vestibule
after I'd already put on my hat and overcoat.

Ding-ding-ding.
"It's a comfort, Myra," Frank hissed.

His fingers around my wrist.
My wrist on the cold metal door.

Ding-ding-ding.
For whom, I wanted to say, *whom does it comfort.*

But I'd forgotten:
Frank worked the mill with Norman.

I took off my hat; I hung my coat back on the rack.
Every night, the sound of those bells:

Ding-ding-ding!
I swallow back the reminder.

Keep-Away Signs

1958 Oral History Interview Project,
A Report for Miss Sophokill's Class by Marcus,
Alma Donovan-Smith's Grandson

Mama wore a gauze mask
in the house

like she read people did
in bigger places like Philly and San Francisco.

In those days, they thought
if you just covered your mouth, you were fine.

Nobody knew where it came from,
how it spread, who was next.

It was a panic.
People put keep-away signs on their front doors.

We didn't visit Mama's cousins
like we did every Sunday.

La Grippe

the headlines called it in New York,
Philadelphia, Peoria, Modesto. A gripe,
achy tremors rattling the joints
like bone plates turned tectonic, crumbling

inside from quiver, from fever, from internal
drowning.

Postmaster

Marv "Rowdy" Doffelmeyer, 1943

It was a warfront.
I'll grant you, the kind without bullets.
But scarier for it.

You just didn't know who was next.

Old Man Dods who trained me,
Ken Simms, one morning sorter,
an afternoon carrier,

boom! Dead. In the matter of a month.

Never seen nothing like it, to this day.
Word came from the governor upstate—
cease and desist delivery.

The last thing I did before locking up

was post a sign on the door:
Closed by state order
until further notice.

That post stayed up for weeks

I venture not more than a dozen saw it
that whole time. People stayed in—
Calloway's Green Grocery, the schools,

even the mill closed.

I'll tell you what, son,
not to have been alive then
your generation is the luckier for it.

Flossie Thornton

She's known this tumbling before:
a barrel with the bottom falling out,
a roil in her gut at all hours.

Should be called
all-day sickness,
she grins

thinking it.
She cannot wait
to tell Walter.

Pennies are tight, but
the boys'll make room
for another.

If it's a girl, she smiles,
I can sew my yellow gingham apron
into a pinafore. Or she can wear Lillian's.

After four sons, she's pretty sure
it won't be,
but she dreamt last night

of pin-curls and ribbons,
Lillian cradling her sister like a dolly.
Again, the trembling kick,

the nausea she swallows back.
Are you trying to tell your mama?
Are you a girl, little one? Hmmm?

Watching out the window
as the boys feed the chicks in the yard,
her palm massages the bitty bump,

a new baby,
while something else
she cannot know

descends,
within her
it unfurls.

Part Three: Good Samaritan

Cure-Alls

"Wear a Mask and Save Your Life! A Mask is 99% Proof Against Influenza." —Full-page newspaper ad, sponsored by the San Francisco Mayor, Red Cross, Chamber of Commerce, and Labor Council

They try:
suspending
from their necks
tiny pouches
of garlic,

onion soup,
onion salads,
onion omelets,
onion syrup,
soaking head-to-toe
in onion baths,

goose grease
poultices,
salt up the nose,
shovels of hot coals
with brown sugar,
a vaporizer
of blue-green smoke,

gargling
boric acid
and sodium bicarbonate,

paper masks
with their noses
still exposed.

From the Limestone Tower

Pastor Glynn

It got to where
in his sleep, Pastor Glynn dreamt
not of the Ladies Auxiliary
shoofly pies cooling in the parsonage
or long summer swims
in Johnston's Lake

but of reaching up for the rope,
the fibrous knot, and the burn
as his grip tugged after
the sonorous sound
that traveled through him
as a lightning strike—
each pull the calling out
from the limestone tower, perched
high above the town treetops
into the dulcet setting sun—
each one, someone's face
he could call up from memory
personally—

Ding—Oden Drake, Mill Worker, 41,

Ding—Miss Virginia Mathers, Primary School Teacher, 23,

Ding—Norman Peters, 30,

Ding—Flossie Thornton, 27.

Picture 100 Recruits: April 21, 1918

Camp Funston, Kansas

Mostly farm boys
just out of school
or quit school to work
or new fathers, faces
still dappled with acne,
one hundred earnest strong
Jacks, Harolds, Johns,
Jims fallen ill in hours.

Forty-eight expire,
and you don't know yet:
one of them will be Brush,
one of them will be you.

Good Samaritan

At the Thorntons, Minerva brought
a loaf of homemade wheat bread
covered with a dishcloth to keep it warm,
minded the children
while Mrs. Thornton thrashed
between quilts.

At the Smiths, Minerva pumped
water from the side yard,
washed dishes, started supper
while Geraldine tended
her husband who took to bed
from the mill
with teeth chattering
before the town shut it down.

At the Donovans, Minerva helped milk
Guernseys, tossed feed to chickens,
pressed cold compresses
to the flushed cheeks
of two of the three sisters.

Without a mask, without quarantining,
Minerva never caught the virus. She lived
until 1947.

Alma

1958 Oral History Interview Project,
A Report for Miss Sophokill's Class by Marcus,
Alma Donovan-Smith's Grandson

The second wave
in 1919 was when I came down with it.
My little sister Eunice got it first.

School shut down for a few weeks.
No going to the store, either.
Main and Park Streets were ghost towns.
Many of us didn't go to the hospital
unless we were really bad off.
Only rich people like the Chandlers
who owned the mill or the Finnleys
whose daddy was the state inspector
had nursing care or went to St. Agnes.

I remember a terrible fever, aches all over
like the regular flu, but more so.
Coughing so hard and hoarse
it rattled in my chest,
made my throat raw.

And the terrible visions!
I thought I saw Eunice's face peel back
to bone.

It Was There in the Schoolyard

Outside Miss Virginia Mathers' classroom,
at the mill, the Presbyterian and Catholic
and Baptist pews, Calloway's Green Grocery,
St. Agnes Hospital,
the Smiths, the Thorntons
when Walter walked in
for Flossie's welcome-home coffee cake,
at the Donovans the week before
when Minerva gathered pails of Guernsey milk.

Minerva

It's what you do.
We all need a hand
now and again.

That Thornton case, though,
that was a sad one.
Not to tell tales on neighbors,

but I went out to the back porch
after Florence passed.
The youngest followed.

"I want my mommy," he said. A wee child,
clinging onto my knee.
I thought of my own mother,

eighteen years gone this summer.
Every day, some sparrow song,
the red ribbon in a girl's hair, something

in me wished she was still here.
You can't tell a child that.
They already know.

I spotted the straw broom
propped by the door. I nested my hands over his
over the handle.

"Let me teach you," I said.
Back and forth we swept
splintered boards that never came clean.

It's what you do.
You give
where you can.

Help

Nurse Noonan

"Miss, miss!" Their spouses call her,
begging to be next, begging for the doctor.
"My mother! My father!" The children
cry, running up to her, pulling
at her dress. "Help, help, help."

Nurse Noonan surveys
the waiting room, their coughs
turning into suffocating gasps—

Margaret Chandler, the mill owner's wife,
wrapped in a mink coat and still shivering,
Ralph Finley's brother, Tucker,
propped against his driver,

Geraldine Smith's husband
part of the overflow in the hallway,
calling "Nurse...I can't...
air...air..."

She knows it won't help.
But she was told. What can she do?

They grab for her wrists,
with barking coughs, gray-blue skin.
Gushing from their noses,
then their mouths,
the ruby spatters begin.

A Hammer and a Spare and a Sack of Sixpenny Nails

Alma Donovan's dad, Philip

Father Costas asked a bunch of us.
Tom Heneckle, Russell Moses, and I
were one of four or five crews
that went down there to the lumberyard
every night for weeks. I took
a hammer and a spare
and a sack of sixpenny nails.

We were given the scraps—oak and ash
with hard knots big as a fist or thick splinters.
We went down there after our mill shifts.
It got pitch dark by five. We had to hurry.
Many nights it snowed.
The iron cold in our nostrils,
our hammers driving nail heads in—
next, next, next until enough

boxes were finished. We loaded them
onto a parish wagon that Tom took over.
He told me once: the bodies in the mortuary
were stacked three abreast in the hallway.
Then laid to rest quick, without services.

What got me were the tiny ones—
no bigger than a doll's bed
like my three daughters used.

Aurelia Glynn, 17

Sometimes I go with him.
I hate to think of him up there, alone.
We climb the stairs,
Dad goes a step behind me,
completely silent
but I count the steps as we go
for something to do, something
 to fill the eerie quiet.

There's a sparrow's nest
in the bell tower, and
some corn husks the wind
must have picked up
and left.

In the tower, the town
looks Tom-Thumb size,
the rooftops—the Smith's,
the Donovan's, the rectory,
the Thornton farmhouse—
become dollhouses,
horses the size of my thumbnail.

I want to reach down
and cup my palm over each house
and lift them up here
with us, cup the ponies in my palm.
Away, almost in the clouds.

But then Dad reaches for the rope.
Ding-ding-ding-ding. His eyes sadden.
Ding-ding-ding-ding. Sadder
than when another knock comes

to the parsonage door. Sadder
than when he steps out
to say what, what does he say
to comfort them?

I can think of nothing;
I forget the quaint housetops, the mini ponies.
The bells never seem to stop.
We can never descend
fast enough to stop my shivering.

Recovery

1958 Oral History Interview Project,
A Report for Miss Sophokill's Class by Marcus,
Alma Donovan-Smith's Grandson

It was a week
before I could sit up in bed
and run a brush through my hair
to sort out the snarls.
Another few days more
until I could walk
across the room
without swaying like a top
or passing out.

Imagine: the feeling
of running water from the pump
heated on the kettle
over my hair. Imagine:
the feeling of running bare feet
across grass just starting to green,
darting across that green
with arms open.

I felt stunned amazement.
Fresh air, running,
life anew—
Lazarus awoken from the tomb.

With a Passing Fever

Nurse Noonan, 1933

Brown, green,
grey, black,
hazel, blue.

Their deadened eyes visit her
in night terrors,
in daydreams,
when holding
her daughter, Stella,
ill with a passing fever
fifteen years later.

1918 was her first year
at St. Agnes. They still had
war shortages then—
never enough doctors and nurses
for shifts; she often worked
thirty-six hours on. Never enough beds
or relief from pain.

Walter Receives a House Call from Pastor George Ashcombe Glynn

How
am I supposed to raise
four sons and Lillian
by myself?

This wasn't the plan.
I got back. I made it through
the trenches, the tear gas,
all that mess.

We were having another one.
Flossie thought
it was a sister for Lillian.
Had started on sewing a dress.
A pretty yellow thing.
How will I raise Lillian?
A girl needs a mother.

How should I answer our five children
when they keep asking
why this happened, where's mommy?
How am I supposed to handle
every day

without her?
I've been with Flossie
since we were fifteen.

It Was There

The virus, it was already there, there, there, there, there, there, there, there.

St. Agnes Hospital

Nurse Noonan

Her heartbeat in her ears.
Her heartbeat in her ears,

in the end
she covers them with thin blankets,
wheels them to the patio,
hurries back for the next.

One Lifetime

1958 Oral History Interview Project,
A Report for Miss Sophokill's Class by Marcus,
Alma Donovan-Smith's Grandson

I'm not sure. I was blessed
or I was one of the lucky ones. Take your pick.
There were others who were as healthy as I was
before it—jumping rope, playing hopscotch,
young mothers and fathers with babies to raise
who didn't survive the fever.

It's not something nice to talk about.

Loving Mother

Florence Mae Thornton
and Unborn Infant
October 27, 1891-
November 2, 1918
27 years, 4 days
Loving Mother,
Wife, Daughter

Psalm 91:
He that dwelleth
in the secret place
of the most High
shall abide
under the shadow
of the Almighty.

Such a Thing

Tom Heneckle, Commemorative Interview,
The Greenfield Gazette, 1928

Those were hard times money-wise,
but what still gets me most—
I lost many good friends,
friends who were like family to me,
folks my kids went to school with,
their parents, even their teacher.
There was no sense to it.

I tell you, though,
the spirit of this town is tough.
We banded together;
we watched out for each other.
We got through it;
may we never have to
get through such a thing again.

Acknowledgments and Historical Notes of Interest

While researching to write this collection, I watched three documentaries that proved invaluable: *America's Forgotten Pandemic: The Influenza of 1918* (Documentary Tube, April 12, 2014), *We Heard the Bells: The Influenza of 1918* (Department of Health and Human Services, January 2010), and *Killer Flu: The Evolution of a Virus (Secrets of the Dead,* PBS, May 6, 2009). Such statistics and quotations as the following sparked my imagination and sympathies at the immense vulnerability and powerlessness this widespread illness caused:

> The influenza pandemic of 1918-1919 killed more people than the Great War, known today as World War I (WWI), at somewhere between 20 and 40 million people. It has been cited as the most devastating epidemic in recorded world history. More people died of influenza in a single year than in four-years of the Black Death Bubonic Plague from 1347 to 1351. Known as "Spanish Flu" or "La Grippe" the influenza of 1918-1919 was a global disaster.

> —Molly Billings, "The Influenza Pandemic of 1918"
> virus/stanford.edu/uda, June 1997

Many of the tragic facts surrounding the pandemic surprised me, including that the virus was adapted from an avian strain. Extreme inflammation often led to suffocation since the virus settled high in the lungs and not in the respiratory tract. There were many reports of the skin of patients turning an eerie blue tinge. The misnomer of Spanish Flu was often given to the virus, but it did not start in Spain, although many scholars agree that WWI trench warfare—with soldiers in such close proximity—undoubtedly helped to spread the flu worldwide. One report I read noted that in the fall of 1918, 500 citizens a week perished in Berlin. India lost almost 4% of its population while the South Seas' death rate was 20%. Ninety percent of an Inuit village perished.

Years ago, I read a beautifully rendered novel by Geraldine Brooks about the Bubonic Plague in Europe, *Year of Wonders: A Novel of the Plague*. That such great devastation could blindside a population while highlighting human capacity for great compassion and great destruction was captivating. I also remember interviewing my paternal grandfather, Joseph Faith, for a middle-school project about the Great Depression and other life events. During the discussion, he mentioned being a young child during America's flu epidemic and the quarantine signs neighbors put on their doors to warn away visitors. For years, these two events lay dormant within my mind and heart as I pursued other writing projects.

As I worked on these poems, I became especially interested in how everyday people deal with adversity and grief in the form of unexpected illness. I also hoped to explore the emotional panic and consequences of the flu pandemic. The 1918 flu was different in that it tended to strike down otherwise-healthy adults in their prime, ages 18-40, compared to outbreaks that target children and the elderly. The pandemic's global and local causes and its connections to both war and animals were unexpected details unearthed while research-ing. After learning of the historically accurate jump-rope rhyme, the first poem in this collection, "Rope," introduced Alma Donovan-Smith and from there, characters' fears, joys, and trials appeared one after the other. It is my hope that this fictional collection, much like Edgar Lee Masters' *Spoon River Anthology,* will encourage those interested in the history of the time period and the potentialities of character development within poetry.

As a side note, while nearing completion on these poems in March 2015, I contracted a flu-like virus; for more than two weeks, I spent many hours in bed aching, coughing, and nauseous. Slowly emerging, I empathized with and ruminated on my characters as if they were living companions, and my heart further went out to the millions of flu-sufferers and their families both in the US and throughout the world who weathered or succumbed to the 1918 pan-demic as well as viruses since.

I wish to thank the following fellow poets whose friendship, encouragement, and suggestions were ongoing and much appreciated while writing these poems: Matt Caretti, Jessie Carty, Joel Griffith, Willie James King, Karen Mason, Valerie Nieman, Elena Arosemena, Susan Beverly, Helen Losse, and Charles Swanson. Many thanks to Diane Kistner and Rachel MacAulay, whose vision and hard work on behalf of my manuscript has made publishing with FutureCycle Press an absolute pleasure. Your dedication to producing high-quality literature for readers is greatly appreciated. I am also deeply in debted to my parents, Linda and Thom Faith, and my sister, Amanda McGrath, and family—Adam, Cora Vi, and Sylvie Ro McGrath—for their continual support and good cheer that sustains me; much love. Many thanks to my writing students in high school (The Mercersburg Academy), university (Southern New Hampshire University's MA in English program), and beyond (Women on Writing! and independent study students) whose curiosity and determination keep me inspired.

Cover *artwork, "Electron micrograph of 1918 influenza strain"*
by Cynthia Goldsmith and Dr. Terrence Tumpey, USCDCP; author
photo by Amanda McGrath; cover and interior book design by
Diane Kistner; Georgia text, Satisfy and Avenir Condensed titling

About FutureCycle Press

FutureCycle Press is dedicated to publishing lasting English-language poetry books, chapbooks, and anthologies in both print-on-demand and Kindle ebook formats. Founded in 2007 by long-time independent editor/publishers and partners Diane Kistner and Robert S. King, the press incorporated as a nonprofit in 2012. A number of our editors are distinguished poets and writers in their own right, and we have been actively involved in the small press movement going back to the early seventies.

The FutureCycle Poetry Book Prize and honorarium is awarded annually for the best full-length volume of poetry we publish in a calendar year. Introduced in 2013, our Good Works projects are anthologies devoted to issues of universal significance, with all proceeds donated to a related worthy cause. Our Selected Poems series highlights contemporary poets with a substantial body of work to their credit; with this series we strive to resurrect work that has had limited distribution and is now out of print.

We are dedicated to giving all of the authors we publish the care their work deserves, making our catalog of titles the most diverse and distinguished it can be, and paying forward any earnings to fund more great books.

We've learned a few things about independent publishing over the years. We've also evolved a unique, resilient publishing model that allows us to focus mainly on vetting and preserving for posterity poetry collections of exceptional quality without becoming overwhelmed with bookkeeping and mailing, fundraising activities, or taxing editorial and production "bubbles." To find out more about what we are doing, come see us at www.futurecycle.org.

The FutureCycle Poetry Book Prize

All full-length volumes of poetry published by FutureCycle Press in a given calendar year are considered for the annual FutureCycle Poetry Book Prize. This allows us to consider each submission on its own merits, outside of the context of a contest. Too, the judges see the finished book, which will have benefitted from the beautiful book design and strong editorial gloss we are famous for.

The book ranked the best in judging is announced as the prize-winner in the subsequent year. There is no fixed monetary award; instead, the winning poet receives an honorarium of 20% of the total net royalties from all poetry books and chapbooks the press sold online in the year the winning book was published. The winner is also accorded the honor of being on the panel of judges for the next year's competition; all judges receive copies of all contending books to keep for their personal library.